URBAN

ROSE

Helle Gade

BUTTERDRAGONS
PUBLISHING

Title: Urban Rose

Author: Helle Gade

Copyright © 2022 Butterdragons® Publishing

All Rights Reserved

Published by Butterdragons® Publishing
https://butterdragons.com

ISBN: 9789493229808 (ebook)
ISBN: 9789493229815 (hardback)
ISBN: 9789493229822 (audio book)

Cover Design by: Dazed Designs

Audio book narrated by Martha Webb

I'm dedicating this book to Raymond and Pedja.

You guys are remarkable.

Just the fact that you hold your own surrounded

by loud females – two legged, furry, and

feathery – is amazing!

Thank you for your eternal patience.

For Helle, with love

We play together in the garden, the Goddess of Poetry and I, and in the brightness of the sunshine, she pauses to let off a poem, presenting it as a gift, especially for me.

Then we pay, I say, for my family are not beggars, we are honoured by the poem, exquisitely crafted in our garden on such an inspirational day, and we shall pay.

I could never ask such a thing of you, she says, I pay, such **a steep price** I pay, there is no recompense possible, for the loss of balance, the emotions encapsulated into each poem, the shearing away.

I listen to the poem three times, feel its **haunting** essence, the sound of the slice of the soul of the Goddess of Poetry, feel it enter my brain, **and** I have to ask her again.

Is it **painful** when the emotion twists and wraps around itself, forms a shard which threatens to tear, to piece it together and slice it away from you?

Yes, it hurts, **yet** as the emotion lives on within the poem, so then, my other emotions can sparkle and enhance themselves in the extra space provided, I feel each more fiercely, until they seem ready to bubble up and then, **we do it again**.

Could I learn to be a poet, my Goddess, could I seek my innermost turmoil and my spirit's fiercest tantalisation, could I squeeze and swirl them together again **and again**, and poof, away comes a poem from me?

I would love to share my gifts, I lay awake each night, **hoping** my poem will inspire others but alas, I cannot teach you to be poet. **This time** my hands are tied.

It is something you become, listen to your inner self, not to me. Share your love and your passion and your art **will be different** than mine. Let your emotions form their shards as they will, learn to shear them from your soul when they are ready and not before.

And so, I practise, and though the price is yet to be determined, I know I shall forever be in your debt.

by BDP Authors

Inspired by Helle Gade's poem The Price from the
collection Dolce Amore

Orion's Sword

Looking at the nebula, Orion's Sword

I cannot help but think

That this is where dreams come from

It is so spectacular to see

That I doubt any human mind

Could conjure that up

Only the Universe possesses the ability

To create something so fantastical

Aches

Why is it that the worst

Pains and aches

Come sneaking in

Under the cover of darkness?

When you lie in bed

And approach sleep

Your body suddenly decides to remind you

That it has many complaints

Pins and needles

Restlessness

Great heaving waves

Subtle jabs

Hot and cold flashes

Sleep flees the mind

In desperation

Leaving me to take

The brunt of it all

As if sleep isn't already

A subtle illusion

Promising you peace and restoration of energy

Yet elusive and draining

Or it tricks you

You fall asleep immediately

When your head hits the pillow

Though when you wake

Fatigue drags at your limbs

And brain fog clouds the mind

Wilted

Once so fresh and beautiful

Their scent intoxicating

Colour and shape enticing

Now wilted and faded

Old and decaying

Their otherworldly beauty forgotten

Broken

Grey spectre

In misty

Remembrance

Tugging the

Heartstrings

Sorrow following

A broken soul

Never forgotten

Burning

The world is burning

While we all sit on our hands

Watching in horror

Wondering why no one

Does anything

You can't extinguish the entire fire

But be the one

That puts out one match

And watch

As others learn by example

It is the only way to salvage

What little soul we have left

Before we wither and die

To be forgotten

Night

The night is my lover
At times, it excites me
At times, it calms me
One thing is for sure
It never fails me

No matter how strong
The sun is during daytime
The night will fall
Shrouding me in darkness

The gentle silver light of the moon
And stars dotting the sky
Is the only light that guides me
Through wilderness of my emotions
Offering a retreat after hectic day

Side Effects

My mind went adrift
In the startling night
As I was staring
Blindly into the darkness

Soft silence
Caressing my ears
Fooling me
Distracting me

I am delirious
Itching
Slightly nauseous
Sweating bullets

Waiting
For the damn side effects
To go away
Or sleep to take over me

Fear sneaking up my spine
Will it disappear?
Will it get worse?
Old memories resurface

Trying not to think
To go with the flow
Focus on something else
Riding out the storm

Twinkling

The stars are too far away
To care about my broken day
Yet I still find comfort
In watching the night sky
Dotted with millions of stars
Light years away
And perhaps long gone
In the grand scheme of things

See Me

See me

For who I am

Not for who

You want me to be

I am too old to change

Nor do I wish to

I am sure

That I'm not finished

Learning

Evolving

Growing

And I will gladly compromise

But I will not change

For anyone

Let alone you

Asylum

The asylum awaits
Darkened beyond belief
By the troubled beings
Walking the white halls

My sanity
Your sanity
No sanity

Only delusions
Hallucinations
Overconfidence

We all walk these halls
Every day
Slowly loosing
One marble at a time

Vulnerable

To the media

The neighbour's opinion

Society's unrealistic demands

Driving us out of our minds

Crossing into madness daily

As we succumb

To the horrendous rules

Of a twisted society

Death in Disguise

Whispers fall from His lips
Counting down the time
Until we finally meet

I hope to greet Him
With open arms
For He is not my enemy

The only thing I fear
Is that I forgot to live my life
For it is so short
That we must enjoy
Whatever time we are dealt

A weariness that sings to Death
Keeping Him close
A comforting presence
So, when the time comes
He will guide me towards Bifrost
Accompanied by fierce Valkyries
Singing songs of my battles

Toxic

Navigating
The toxic wasteland
Of my pain filled mind
Is a one-way trip
To the fiery depths
Of a shadowy Hell

Sometimes

Watching the candlelight flicker

From my old bed of doom

My vision hazy

The pain continuously throbs in my lower back

I'm deadly tired, but sleep is far away

Fleeing from the constant ache

Meanwhile, I am fighting the misery

Trying desperately to keep my lucidity

And not be swallowed up

By the wretchedness of it all

I am not a fatalistic person

I am not a perfect person, either

Sometimes, I need to allow myself

To wallow in the despair of it all

So, I can crawl out of bed in the morning

With a tiny hope that this day will be better

Wrath

I carry my anger

Hidden from mortal eyes

A supernova waiting to blow

Sometimes it seeps into my thoughts

Darkening them with its poison

Impossible for me to escape

For its hunger knows no bounds

Once unleashed

I fear it will enslave me

Lovers

Tear me apart
Coat me in your darkness

Show me the black corners
Of your jaded soul

I'll be your light in the night
Your shade in the sun

Redemption I am not
I carry my own abyss

I could swallow you up
Instead, I'll share your madness

I'll drink your horror
As you will accept my pain

Envy

The green-eyed critter

Who lives within us all

He rears his ugly head

At the most inconvenient times

I find him stroking my ego

With his cool fingers

Poking it to get a response

That's when the thoughts appear

Why can't I do that?

Why am I not that pretty?

Why am I not that lucky?

We all know him

He sneaks in like a burglar

Placing insecurities

That fester in our minds

And corrupt our thoughts

Chance

The captivating honeysuckle

Ensnares you

With its sensual scent

Seduces you

Of the beaten path

Towards hidden treasures

Or certain death

Take the chance

Walk the path

Feel the pain

Wolf Words

You are a wolf
In sheep's clothing
Spouting pretty words
Utter nonsense
Flowery prose
Lies in disguise

You think me
Fooled
Laughing
Behind my back
Telling tales
Of my ignorance

But be warned
I know your tricks
There will be no pardon
I will purge you
From my body
And certainly, my mind

Affliction

It is here again
Creeping in there
Under the cover of nightfall

Causing hell in the system
Keeping sleep away

Streaming through
My delicate nerves
Right below the skin

My aching muscles
Full of unrest

The discomfort
Persistent and unwanted

I am a vasal of this affliction

Incarcerated
In this mortal part

Doomed to endure
More than most
Yet less than many

Restlessness and agony
My escorts through life

A teaching experience
I could do without
But have to welcome
So it will not own me

World of Love

I feel their love

Crossing the Arctic Circle

Melting the ice on their way

Flowing by Equator

Bringing the warmth

Of exotic places

It doesn't matter

If they look at

The Northern Star

Or the Southern Cross

Their love feels the same

When I need it the most

Borders are torn down

As they reach out to me

Through currents in the air

Their energies embracing me

Friendship and love

Freak Show

Ladies and gentlemen
I give to you my heart

This cardiovascular muscle
Filled with flaws
Stitched together
More times than I can count

Ripped out of my chest
Yet still beating

Behold the freakish organ
As it huffs and puffs
Trying to vanquish pain
But bleeding endlessly

Golden Thread

I spy the golden thread
That ties you to me
I wonder if it will ever
Dissolve or be cut
So, I yet again
Can be free

I am bound
Tighter and tighter
Day by day
Yearning to be loose
To run with bare feet
In dew covered grass
Towards the rising sun

Hope incarnate
Look upon me
With gentle eyes
I know I am not
Without faults
But I beg of you
To have mercy

I try ever so hard
To live up to expectations
Though they are harsh
And painful

Let your touch be gentle
And voice hushed
Then I will be
Forever grateful

Demise

Those empty sockets

Staring at me

Begging

Condemning

Questioning

I cannot escape

Enthralled

Frozen in my seat

Awaiting

Final judgement

Malicious

A tear along the seam
Stitches broken
Heart ripped
By one word

A virulent feeling
Malignant intention
Said with insolent glee

Repeat

As the days go by
The dreams take flight
Routines are repeated
Creating a mind-numbing effect
Wasting my precious life

Where did the dreams go?
Were they ever a possibility?

Or am I doomed to live out life
Unable to fulfil those dreams
So, I burry them in tedious tasks
Preformed in an unending circle

A Bite

Bittersweet reminiscence

Consigned to oblivion

By a bite

Conjuring delightful amnesia

The only thought

Is the velvety feel on the tongue

Run

Run

Run

The hunter is here
Run for your life
Protect yourself
Run with all your might
For he will chase you
Mercilessly
Until he holds your heart

He will hold it gently at first
Caressing it lovingly
Bringing warmth and safety
But eventually
He will grow bored
Yearning for the chase
He will throw it away
Moving on without a thought
Beyond his precious hunt

Nightly Travels

My dreams take me
Far and wide

From the horrors of the Abyss
To the fields Elysium

I bathe in starlight
And burn in hellfire

Yet, I would do it
Again and again

To feel it all
To feel alive

The Ledge

Choose the light
Choose me

Why is the ledge
So terribly tempting?

I can make you smile
I know I can

Let me sit with you
When the hurt is overwhelming

Let me listen
When you need to talk

Ask me for help
And I'll be there

Ugly Feelings

Fingers leaving patterns of betrayal

Their path unyielding

Pulling forth ugly feelings

That should have been forgotten

But now rising to the surface

A tsunami of heartache

Drowning me without stealth

Time

Tik tok

Tik tok

Never enough

Always running

Freeze

Breathe

Shake it off

Gaze at the stars

Learn to be present

No more rushing

Towards an early grave

Watch the moon

Travel over the sky

Rejoice when the first light

Peaks above the horizon

Taste the morning dew

Dance wildly in the rain

And be yourself, whoever you are

Don't get lost in the crowd

Moving

I cannot do it anymore
Up and down
The creaking sounds
The pain
It is a dreadful realisation
Having to admit my limitations
I ignored my body for as long as I could
I truly had myself fooled

It is a hard truth to swallow
That I have to leave the place I love
It has been my security blanket
For more years than I want to admit
My personal comfort zone
Where I could hide and recuperate
Yet still feel like I belong
Without having to interact

I am shaken to my core
Adrenaline is coursing through my body
I am on the verge of tears
I cannot catch my breath
A panic attack
Yes, that is what this is
Breath in
Breath out

I know that I will make a new cave
A place where I feel safe
A new life with more possibilities
Of doing what I humbly dream of
But until I get there, chaos will rule
I will spit and growl
I will run around like a madwoman
Not accomplishing much

Spring Sun

The sun has once again
Escaped my greedy claws
She hid behind the clouds
And sent the fog to disorientate me

I fiercely need her warmth
To heat my frozen body
And melt my heart

I need an awakening of my soul
From its wintertime slumber
I am ready to emerge from the soil
And unfold my green leaves

The dark and frosty season
Needs to make way
For the birth of spring

Magic is waiting to explode
In bright colours
That dazzle the eye

Please, my Lady

Grace us with your glorious presence

Show us that there is love and joy to behold

In the nature, as well as in our hearts

The Path

Old memories
And faded dreams
Line a path behind me
Hazy fog
And half promises
Cover the path before me

I feel as though I stand still
Yet, I move fast along the path
Stumbling my way forward
And climbing over obstacles
Feeling like a rat
In a maze full of dead ends

Bully

Simple words

Can pierce the thickest skin

Be it love or hate

Intentional or not

They can build you up

And tear you down

Creeping slowly under the skin

Or thrown in your face

Think before you speak

You might not be aware

That people feel bullied

By what you consider fun

Migraine

The mother of all headaches
Has taken root in my skull
She starts out with a gentle tapping
Looking for the weak spots
The fault lines of the cranium

As she grows more confident
She proceeds to hammering
Sending sharp stabs of pain
Bouncing of my skull walls

Then she unleashes the storm
Lighting blinding my eyes
Thunder roaring in my ears
A continuous throbbing in my head
Feeling like my brain is too big
For my small cranium

Nausea follows the storm

Causing fear of vomiting

Which would only make the storm worse

Crawling towards cool darkness

To try and calm her wrath

Every move causing excruciating pain

To pummel my mind and slow my step

Reborn

Star born

From eternal fire

Hardening

Heart and soul

Stepping out of the flames

To take her place

In the world, yet again

Wiser and stronger

Judgment

Why should we hide in the shadows

Ashamed of things beyond our control?

We have not chosen this life

No one would choose it

You strip us of our dignity

And punish us for our pain

You bring chaos into our lives

When all we need is calm

You judge us and call us lazy

Thinking yourselves better than us

Right up until it happens to you

Because no matter who you are

It can hit you at any point in life

Remember that the next time

You sit on your high horse and judge us

For something beyond our control

Yearning

My desires carry me wide and far
Unknown yearning blossoming
Inside my ribcage

I follow the feeling
Until I am spread so thin
That I bounce back painfully

Everything instantly forgotten
Like a delicate scent
Of a flower on my path

Yet it won't hold me back
Should the desire bloom again
Stretching my being to its limits

Words of Wisdom

Illuminate me

Throw me your fickle words

Of one-sided wisdom

It obviously makes you feel better

Superior even

It must be nice

To think you know it all

To feel so sure

Of your place in this world

That you feel you have the right

To dictate me

How I should live my life

Burning Sky

The sky is burning
Flames parting the clouds
Illuminating the earth below

Stars rain down
As if the Universe
Is crying diamond tears

Heat and ashes
Twirling through the air
Suffocating

The end is near
Yet, I do not fear it
For it is time to let
Mother Earth rest

White Silence

White all around me
Moisture in the air I breathe
The wind is a cold caress
Chilling me inside and out

But luckily, the sun prevails
Carving holes in the white wall
Showing me glimpses of gentle giants
Resting side by side

They watch the time go by
With agonizing slowness
Eons of history
Buried in their memories

No rush here
The only sounds
The tinkling of a tiny stream
Or a bell here and there

Want

I want to bask in the glory

Of a single word

Whispered by a lover

I want to be owned

And to own someone

To know their deepest secrets

And not be afraid to share mine

I want to be held when I am hurting

To have someone sharing

The joy of the happy days

But the fear always holds me back

I know that I deserve love

But thinking that no one deserves

To put up with my illness

Thinking about how I will never be able

To keep up with a healthy person

Yet not have the energy

To be with a sick person

So, I stand back and watch the world

Living vicariously

Through family and friends

Cold Pain

Silver slivers of pain

Radiating frost through my bones

Glacier melting down my spine

A snowstorm that threatens

To rip the flesh of my bones

Hoar frost coating my lungs

Threatening to choke me

Malady

A beast lives inside me

A growling clawing beast

Ripping and tearing my insides

Furious to get out

At least, that is how it feels

There is no place it leaves alone

No place sacred from its attacks

It is a malady I cannot escape

Dark Ladies

Ladies of the night

Flying above the clouds

Swathed in murder and mayhem

Their hunger for blood

Legendary amongst the stars

Feared by all on earth

For they are the unwilling givers

Of their life's blood

Of their last breath

A dark price to pay

For the dark protection

Against these fallen angles

Phantom

He is a phantom
Haunting my dreams
With smoky touches
Over my bare skin

He is my chimera
Mine to chase
Through my imagination
Until I wake

Each day I long
For the endless night
Where I can pursue
Another touch from him

Restlessness

A constant unrest
Torments my body
Torments my soul
When the darkness descends

The balance is broken
Thoughts crowding my head
And madness lurks
Right around the corner

Yet another night
Spent awake
Mourning the lost sleep
The lost sanity

Please

My heart is out there

Take a look

I care not for your judgement

Only your compassion

Do not throw me away

For past sins that have been forgiven

Embrace me for who I am now

But if you cannot

Then be silent and walk away

Agreement

67

He demands my obedience

He demands my consent

As he plays my body

Like an instrument of pain

Unique

Save me from this mortal sin

Release me

Let me fly free of this judgement

Their rationality is flawed

Colouring me grey

Absorbing my precious energy

In a mass of indistinguishable people

Transforming me into one of millions

Instead of a unique individual

Colourful and joyous

No more

Online Breakdown

It feels like the tears are still there
Waiting to burst out
Staining my cheeks with their salt

I am unhinged, fractured
A thousand-piece puzzle
That is broken down

Yet, you all are still here
Picking up the pieces
Spread all over the world

I feel your love
As your words slowly mend
The shattered feeling inside

I wish I could express
The extent of my gratitude

Betrayal

Hurry up and run
Before the sky opens up
Ready to swallow you whole
For the betrayal of my heart

It would have been easier
For you to stab me
Instead of relying on elaborate lies
And subterfuge

But don't you worry
Karma never forgets
And neither do I
So, hurry up and run

Bliss

Pleasure

Is a dream

That comes before heartache

A longing

So very

Strong

It consumes

The lonely heart

Like a burning sun

Driving us

Towards each other

In a frantic dance

Seeking solace

Where none is to be found

Yet, we desperately keep trying

The Mask

Let me rip of my mask of humanity
And show you the evil that lies beneath
It will rip you apart
And not shed a tear about it

Whereas I, with my mask on
I'll say yes, and apologize till the end
A quivering mass of excuses

Let me show you the truth
That resides in my broken soul
Let me infect you with my malice
Then we can both simmer in the pain

Sleepless

73

When Sandman denies me his presence
And Morpheus ignore my pleas
Insanity slowly crawls forward
A maddening feeling

The desire to sleep is overwhelming
It clutches your mind
Crushing it

Empathy

I see your darkness
In a black cloud
Surrounding your being

I hear your pain
In the silence
You carry it like a shield

I feel the anxiety
In the way your body
Trembles ever so slightly

I understand the cry for help
From the tears in your eyes
I am here for you!

Dying Sun

75

As I stood and looked
Into the centre of a dying sun
My heart wept golden tears

So much life soon to be lost
Leaving a cold black void
Begging to be filled

By a new light
By a new warmth
By new life

Reckless

I miss being reckless

Doing things in the spur of the moment

There is no longer room for spontaneity

Yet, I can hardly follow a schedule

Without feeling restrained by appointments

I drift through the days

My eyes shaded

My hearing muffled

Awash in a cloud of pain

That burns through my whole body

Like a dragon searching for treasure

I admit out loud that I have accepted it

As if that will help make it true

But I am lying to myself

A lifetime of indoctrination by society's rules

Takes a lifetime to change

Despite of what I try telling myself

I fight for some kind of control

Any kind of control, for that matter

And that is what I am denied

What I wouldn't do to lie back

And go with the flow

Careless of any demands

Stolen

My heart was stolen
On a cold night
A thief snuck in
Grabbed the bloody thing
I could hear the thump, thump
As he ran away with it

Empty
Hollow
Missing

Its cavity in my chest
Is cold and hurting
The missing thump, thump
Is deafening
My blood turned to ice
My soul covered in hoar frost

I await springtime

Hoping there is a seed

Waiting to unfold

To thaw me

Perhaps I will hear

A silent thump

And then another

Destroy

You destroy me with your kindness

Why can you not understand that?

I hate the pity in your voice

Why would you think I would appreciate that?

Do not talk to me as if I am a child

Would you like me to talk to you that way?

I am in pain and mentally exhausted

I need you to be strong and say

Yeah, it sucks, here's some chocolate

The pity demeans me

It takes away my humanity

I Wish

I wish to be the cool moon in the darkness
Which you gaze upon as you rest for the night

I wish to be the dawn
That wakes you from your slumber

I wish to be your sun
To be the heat that sustains you

I wish to be the dusk that reminds you
That it is time to rest in my arms

I wish to be the stars reflected in your eyes
As you gaze upon me

Stalked

Crushing blackness surrounding me
Not a whisper to be heard
Not a breeze to be felt

Alone in this desolate space
Confined in my twisted mind
A captive of my imagination

I cannot escape
It nips at my heels
Hunting me relentlessly

This darkness contains
All my fears
Ready to unleash them on me

Now

Slow languorous days
Under the soft sun
Basking in your love

You brush my heart
With phantom fingers
Making my dreams come true

I love you now
In this moment
Without hesitation

No future
No past
Just the present

Ira

She came into my life
Teaching me to live again

To enjoy the little things
And ask for help when needed

She showed me
The meaning of friendship
And rekindled my taste for life

My Cage

My golden cage

The one place

I should treat with care

Honour and love

That is what I destroy

I break it down

Bit by bit

Mentally and physically

Until I only see

A shrivelled-up carcass

Swaying back and forth

In a desolate place

The Joy

The joy of walking in the park
Beneath the spring-green trees
Without my eternal shadow
Prowling behind me
Like a thief in the night

The joy of standing still
Listening to the wind
Rustling in the treetops
Without having to hurry home
Because my shadow demands it

The joy of feeling
The white flower petals
Rain down on my face
Without feeling my shadows
Breathe on my neck

The joy of coming home
And not having to spend
The rest of the day
Exhausted on my couch
Because my shadow won again

Terrorism

The world is at war
I cry hollow tears
For all the innocents
That move in the path
Of the darkest destruction

The blood runs freely
Soaking the streets
A reminder
Of how precious life is

So, take your loved ones
Hug them hard
And tell them
All that is left unsaid
Show them love

My Girls

They make me laugh until my belly aches
While we speak in tongues

Pure understanding flows between us
As the rest of the world looks upon us
In utter confusion

They are my rocks in hell and high waters
Always there, always understanding

Thank you my sweet friends
You own a piece of my heart

Acknowledgements

I would like to thank the usual suspects Ira, Kim, Sonja, Ben and my readers. You all make this journey easier.

About Helle Gade

Helle Gade lives in Denmark. She is a book blogger, poet, photographer, nocturnal creature, avid reader and chocolate addict. She has been writing poetry since 2011 and published four poetry collections since then. She has been fortunate to work with a bunch of brilliant authors and photographers on The Mind's Eye series. Her book Nocturnal Embers won the Best Poetry Collection with eFestival of Words.

Other BDP books by Helle Gade

Terrifying Love - A Halloween Anthology

Beautiful Tragedy - A Halloween Anthology

How To Tame A Wild Tempest

Poesi - A Collection of Poems Volume One

The Fighter

Spirit

Golden Tattoo - A Halloween Anthology

www.ingramcontent.com/pod-product-compliance
Lightning Source LLC
LaVergne TN
LVHW091356210726
843527LV00001B/25